SONGS & BALLADS
— OF —
IRELAND

A FIRST COLLECTION OF 40 IRISH SONGS
WITH COMPLETE WORDS, MUSIC AND GUITAR CHORDS

Ossian

Printed at Watermans Printers, Cork, for
OSSIAN PUBLICATIONS,
PO BOX 84,
CORK, IRELAND

ISBN 0 946005 53 2
OMB 76

Contents

The Cliffs of Dooneen

You may tra-vel far, far, from your own na-tive home, Far a - way o'er the

moun-tains, far a - way o'er the foam, But of all the fine pla-ces that I've e-ver

been, Oh, there's none___ can com - pare with the Cliffs of Doo - neen.___

It's a nice place to be on a fine summer's day,
Watching all the wild flowers that ne'er do decay,
Oh, the hare and the pheasant are plain to be seen,
Making homes for their young round the Cliffs of Dooneen.

Take a view o'er the mountains, fine sights you'll see there;
You'll see the high rocky mountains on the west coast of Clare,
Oh, the towns of Kilkee and Kilrush can be seen,
From the high rocky slopes round the Cliffs of Dooneen.

So fare thee well to Dooneen, fare thee well for a while,
And although we are parted by the raging sea wild,
Once again I will wander with my Irish colleen,
Round the high rocky slopes of the Cliffs of Dooneen.

5

OMB 76

The Blacksmith

A black-smith cour-ted me, nine months and bet-ter___ He
fair-ly won my heart, wrote me a let-ter___ With his
ham-mer in his hand, he looked so cle-ver___ And if
I was with my love I'd live for-e-ver.___

And where is my love gone, with his cheeks like roses,
And his good black billycock on, decked with primroses,
I'm afraid the scorching sun will shine and burn his beauty,
And if I was with my love, I'd do my duty.

Strange news is come to town, strange news is carried,
Strange news flies up and down that my love is married.
I wish them both much joy, though they don't hear me,
And may God reward him well, for slighting of me.

What did you promise, love, when you sat beside me,
You said you would marry me and not deny me.
'If I said I'd marry you, it was only for to try you,
So bring your witness love, and I'll ne'er deny you.'

Oh witness have I none, save God Almighty,
And He'll reward you well for the slighting of me,
Her lips grew pale and white, it made her poor heart tremble,
To think she loved one and he proved deceitful.

The Bantry Girls' Lament

Oh, who will plough the field now, or who will sell the corn? Oh,
who will wash the sheep now and have them nice-ly shorn? The
stack that's in the hag-gard, un-trash'd it may re-main. Since
John-ny went a-trash-ing the dir-ty king of Spain.

The girls from the bawnoge in sorrow may retire,
And the piper and his bellows may go home and blow the fire;
For Johnny, lovely Johnny, is sailing o'er the Main,
Along with other patriots, to fight the King of Spain.

The boys will sorely miss him when Moneymore comes round,
And grieve that their bold captain is nowhere to be found.
The peelers must stand idle against their will and grain,
For the valiant boy who gave them work now peels the King of Spain.

At wakes or hurling-matches your like we'll never see,
Till you come back to us again, a stoirin óg mo chroí,
And won't you trounce the buckeens that show us much disdain,
Because our eyes are not so bright as those you'll meet in Spain.

If cruel fate will not permit our Johnny to return,
His heavy loss we Bantry girls will never cease to mourn.
We'll resign ourselves to our sad lot, and die in grief and pain,
Since Johnny died for Ireland's pride in the foreign land of Spain.

OMB 76

The Fields of Athenry

By Pete St John

By the lone - ly pri - son wall._____ I

heard a young girl call - - ing

Mi - chael, they are ta - king you a - way,_____ For you

stole Tre - vel - yn's corn. So the young might see_ the morn. Now a

pri - son ship lies wait - ing in the bay._____

Chorus Low, lie the Fields_____ of A - then - ry, where

once we watched the small free birds fly._____ Our_

love was on the wing, We had dreams and songs to sing. It's so

lone - ly 'round the fields of A - then - ry._____

By a lonely prison wall
I heard a young man calling,
Nothing matters Mary when you're free,
Against the Famine and the Crown,
I rebelled they ran me down,
Now you must raise our child with dignity.

By a lonely harbour wall
She watched the last star falling
And that prison ship sailed out against the sky.
Sure she'll wait and hope and pray
For her love in Botany Bay,
It's so lonely round the fields of Athenry.

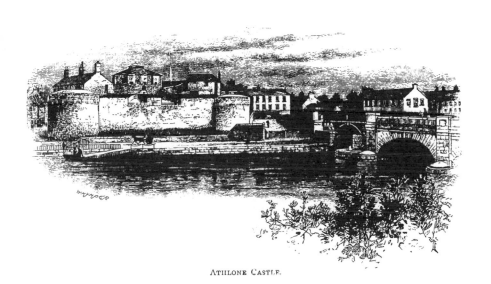

ATHLONE CASTLE.

OMB 76

Spancil Hill

Last night as I lay dream - ing of plea - sant days gone by, Me
mind bein' bent on ram - bling to Ire - land I did fly, I
stepped a - board a vi - sion and fol - lowed with my will, Till
next I came to an - chor at the cross near Span - cil Hill.___

Delighted by the novelty, enchanted with the scene,
Where in my early boyhood where often I had been.
I thought I heard a murmur and I think I hear it still,
It's the little stream of water that flows down Spancil Hill.

It being the twenty-third of June, the day before the fair,
When Ireland's sons and daughters in crowds assembled there.
The young, the old, the brave and the bold, they came for sport and kill,
There were jovial conversations at the cross of Spancil Hill.

I went to see my neighbours, to hear what they might say,
The old ones were all dead and gone, the others turning grey.
I met with tailor Quigley, he's as bold as ever still,
Sure he used to make my britches when I lived in Spancil Hill.

I paid a flying visit to my first and only love,
She's white as any lily and gentle as a dove.
She threw her arms around me, saying 'Johnny, I love you still'
She's Mag, the farmer's daughter and the pride of Spancil Hill.

I dreamt I stooped and kissed her as in the days of yore,
She said 'Johnny, you're only joking, as many's the time before.'
The cock crew in the morning, he crew both loud and shrill,
And I woke in California, many miles from Spancil Hill.

Peggy Gordon

Oh, Peg - gy Gor - don, you are my dar - ling,
Come sit you down u - pon my knee and tell to
me The ve - ry rea - son Why I am
sligh - ted so by thee.

Oh, Peggy Gordon, you are my darling,
Come sit you down upon my knee
And tell to me the very reason
Why I am slighted so by thee.

I wish I was in some lonesome valley,
Where womankind cannot be found,
Where the little birds sing upon the branches,
And every moment a different sound.

Oh, Peggy Gordon, you are my darling,
Come sit you down upon my knee
And tell to me the very reason
Why I am slighted so by thee.

I'm so in love that I can't deny it,
My heart lies smothered in my breast,
But it's not for you to let the world know it,
A troubled mind can know no rest.

I put my head to a cask of brandy,
It was my fancy, I do declare,
For when I'm drinking, I'm always thinking,
And wishing Peggy Gordon was here.

OMB 76

The Spanish Lady

As I went down to Dublin city, at the hour of twelve at night,

Who should I see but a Spanish lady, washing her feet by candle light,

First she washed them, then she dried them, over a fire of amber coal, In

all my life I ne'er did see a maid so sweet about the sole,

Chorus

Whack fol the too-ra,__ loo-ra, laddy, Whack fol the too-ra loo-ra-lay.

Repeat Chorus

As I came back through Dublin city
At the hour of half past eight
Who should I spy but the Spanish lady
Brushing her hair in the broad daylight.
First she tossed it, then she brushed it,
On her lap was a silver comb
In all my life I ne'er did see
A maid so fair since I did roam.

As I went back through Dublin city
As the sun began to set
Who should I spy but the Spanish lady
Catching a moth in a golden net.
When she saw me then she fled me
Lifting her petticoat over her knee
In all my life I ne'er did see
A maid so shy as the Spanish Lady.

I've wandered north and I've wandered south
Through Stonybatter and Patrick's Close
Up and around the Gloster Diamond
And back by Napper Tandy's house.
Old age has laid her hand on me
Cold as a fire of ashy coals
In all my life I ne'er did see
A maid so sweet as the Spanish Lady.

If I was a Blackbird

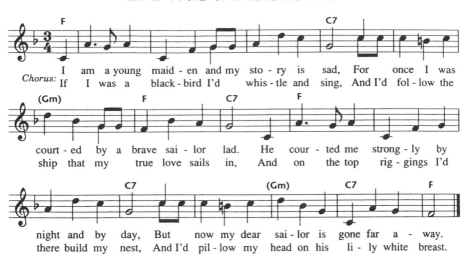

I am a young maid - en and my sto - ry is sad, For once I was
Chorus: If I was a black - bird I'd whis - tle and sing, And I'd fol - low the

court - ed by a brave sai - lor lad. He cour - ted me strong - ly by
ship that my true love sails in, And on the top rig - gings I'd

night and by day, But now my dear sai - lor is gone far a - way.
there build my nest, And I'd pil - low my head on his li - ly white breast.

He promised to take me to Donnybrook fair
To buy me red ribbon to bind up my hair.
And when he'd return from the ocean so wide,
He'd take me and make me his own loving bride.

His parents they slight me and will not agree
That I and my sailor married should be.
But when he comes home I will greet him with joy
And I'll take to my bosom my dear sailor boy.

Cork Harbor.

OMB 76

The Rare Oul' Times

By Pete St John

Based on songs and sto - ries, he - roes of re - known.___ Are the

pas - sing tales and glo - ries, that once was Du - blin town. The

hal - lowed halls and hou - ses, the haunt - ing chil - dren's rhymes. That

once was part of Du - blin, in the rare___ old times.

Chorus

Ring - a - ring - a - Ro - sie, as the light de - clines, I re -

mem - ber Du - blin ci - ty in the rare___ oul' times.

My name it is Sean Dempsey, as Dublin as can be,
Born hard and late in Pimlico, in a house that ceased to be.
By trade I was a cooper, lost out to redundancy.
Like my house that fell to progress, my trade's a memory.
And I courted Peggy Dignan, as pretty as you please,
A rogue and child of Mary, from the rebel Liberties.
I lost her to a student chap, with skin as black as coal.
When he took her off to Birmingham, she took away my soul.

The years have made me bitter, the gargle dims my brain,
'Cause Dublin keeps on changing, and nothing seems the same.
The Pillar and the Met. have gone, the Royal long since pulled down,
As the great unyielding concrete, makes a city of my town.

Fare thee well, sweet Anna Liffey, I can no longer stay,
And watch the new glass cages, that spring up along the Quay.
My mind's too full of memories, too old to hear new chimes,
I'm part of what was Dublin, in the rare ould times.

St. Stephen's Green—North Side.

OMB 76

My Johnny was a Shoemaker

His jacket was a deep sky blue and curly was his hair
His jacket was a deep sky blue, it was I do declare
For to reef the topsails up again the mast
And sail across the stormy sea, e . . ee, e . . ee
And sail upon the deep blue sea.

Some day he'll be a captain bold, with a brave and gallant crew
Some day he'll be a captain bold, with a sword and spy-glass too
And when he has a gallant captain's sword
He'll come home and he'll marry me, e . . ee, e . . ee
He'll come home and he'll marry me.

In Dublin's Fair City

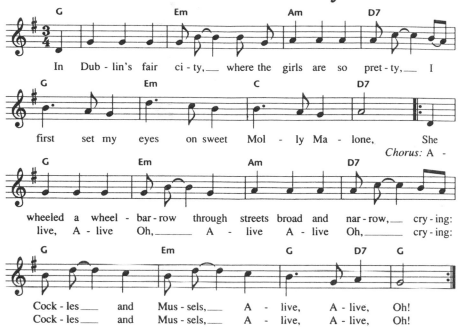

In Dub-lin's fair ci-ty,__ where the girls are so pret-ty,__ I first set my eyes on sweet Mol-ly Ma-lone, She

Chorus: A-

wheeled a wheel-bar-row through streets broad and nar-row,__ cry-ing:
live, A-live Oh,_____ A-live A-live Oh,_____ cry-ing:

Cock-les__ and Mus-sels,__ A-live, A-live, Oh!
Cock-les__ and Mus-sels,__ A-live, A-live, Oh!

She was a fishmonger, but sure 'twas no wonder,
For so were her father and mother before;
And they both wheeled their barrow, through streets broad and narrow,
Crying: 'Cockles and Mussels a-live, a-live oh.'

She died of a fever, no one could relieve her
And that was the end of sweet Molly Malone,
But her ghost wheels her barrow, through streets broad and narrow,
Crying: 'Cockles and Mussels a-live, a-live oh.'

OMB 76

Danny Boy

By F. Weatherly

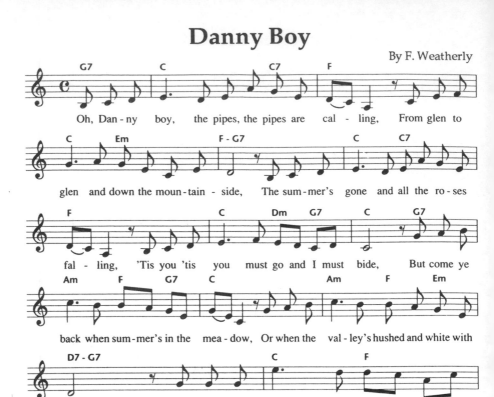

Oh, Dan - ny boy, the pipes, the pipes are cal - ling, From glen to glen and down the moun - tain - side, The sum - mer's gone and all the ro - ses fal - ling, 'Tis you 'tis you must go and I must bide, But come ye back when sum - mer's in the mea - dow, Or when the val - ley's hushed and white with snow. 'Tis I'll be there in sun - shine or in sha - dow, Oh Dan - ny boy, Oh Dan - ny boy I love you so.

And when you come and all the flowers are dying
If I am dead - as dead I well may be,
Ye'll come and find a place where I am lying,
And kneel and say an Ave there for me;
And I shall hear though soft your tread above me,
And all my grave shall warmer, sweeter be,
For you will bend and tell me that you love me,
And I shall live in peace until you come to me.

Avondale

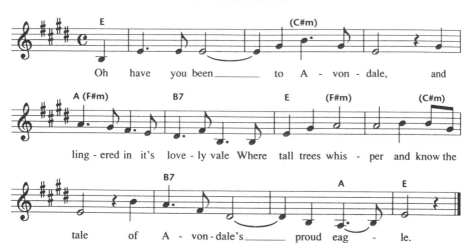

Oh have you been to A - von - dale, and ling - ered in it's love - ly vale Where tall trees whis - per and know the tale of A - von - dale's proud eag - le.

Where pride and ancient glory fade,
So was the land where he was laid
Like Christ was thirty pieces paid
For Avondale's proud eagle.

Long years that green and lovely vale
Has nursed Parnell, her grandest Gael
And curse the land that has betrayed
Fair Avondale's proud eagle.

A Village on Achill.

OMB 76

Where my Eileen is Waiting

I am al - ways light - heart - ed and ea - sy, not a care in the world have I,___ For I know I am loved by a col - leen, and I could not for - get if I tried,___ She lives far a - way o'er the moun - tain, where the lit - tle bids sing on the trees,___ In a cot - tage all co - vered with i - vy,___ My Ei - leen is wai - ting for me,___ It's o - ver, it's o - ver the moun - tain,___ where the lit - tle birds sing on the trees,___ In a cot - tage all co - vered with i - vy,___ my Ei - leen is wai - ting for me.

The time I bade goodbye to Eileen,
Is a time I will never forget,
For the tears bubbled up from their slumbers,
I fancy I see them yet.
They looked like the pearls in the ocean,
As she wept her tale of love,
And she said 'My dear boy don't forget me,
Till we meet here again or above'.

CHORUS, *finishing with a repeat of the last two lines:*
In a cottage all covered with ivy,
My Eileen is waiting for me.

Twenty-One Years

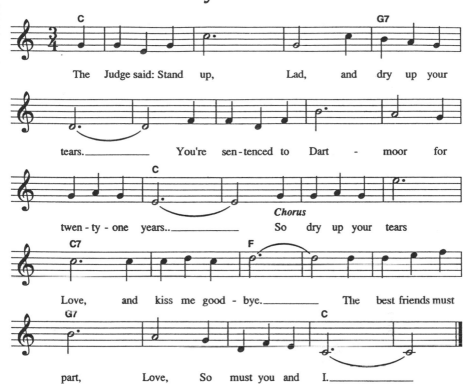

The Judge said: Stand up, Lad, and dry up your tears.____ You're sen-tenced to Dart - moor for twen-ty-one years..____

Chorus

So dry up your tears Love, and kiss me good - bye.____ The best friends must part, Love, So must you and I.____

I hear the train coming, 'twill be here at nine.
To take me to Dartmoor to serve up my time.
I look down the railway and plainly I see,
You standing there waving your goodbyes to me.

Six months have gone by, love, I wish I were dead.
This dark dreary dungeon and stone for my bed.
It's hailing, it's raining, the moon gives no light.
Now won't you tell me, love, why you never write?

I've counted the days, love, I've counted the nights,
I've counted the footsteps, I've counted the lights,
I've counted the raindrops, I've counted the stars,
I've counted a million of these prison bars.

I've waited, I've trusted, I've longed for the day,
A lifetime, so lonely, now my hair's turning grey.
My thoughts are for you, love, till I'm out of my mind,
For twenty-one years is a mighty long time.

21

I Know Where I'm Going

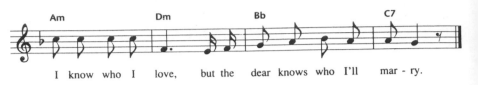

I know where I'm go-ing, and I know who's go-ing with me

I know who I love, but the dear knows who I'll mar-ry.

I'll have stockings of silk,
Shoes of fine green leather,
Combs to buckle my hair
And a ring on every finger.

Feather beds are soft
Painted rooms are bonny;
But I'd leave them all
To go with my love Johnny.

Some say he's dark
I say he's bonny,
He's the flower of them all
My handsome, coaxing Johnny.

I know where I'm going
I know who's going with me,
I know who I love,
But the dear knows who I'll marry.

My Love's an Arbutus

My love's an ar - bu - tus. By the bor - ders of Lene. So slen - der and shape - ly, In her gir - dle of green, And I mea - sure the plea - sure, Of her eye's sap - phire sheen By the blue skies that spar - kle. Through that soft branch - ing.

But though ruddy the berry and snowy the flower,
That brighten together the arbutus bower,
Perfuming and blooming through sunshine and shower,
Give me her bright lips and her laugh's pearly dower.

Alas! fruit and blossom shall lie dead on the lea,
And time's jealous fingers dim your young charms, Machree,
But unranging, unchanging you'll still cling to me,
Like the evergreen leaf to the arbutus tree.

OMB 76

The Skillet Pot

Did you e - ver eat Col - can - non, made from

love - ly pick - led cream?___ With the flour and scal - lions blend - ed like a

pic - ture in a dream.___ Did you e - ver make a hole on top to

hold the melt - ing flake.___ Of the cream - y flav' - ry but - ter that your

Chorus

moth - er used to make? Yes you did, so you

did, so did he and so did I.___ And the more I think a -

bout it sure the near - er I'm to cry.___ Oh, was - n't it the

hap - py days when troub - les we had not___And our moth - ers made Col -

can - non in the lit - tle skil - let pot.___

Yes you did, so you did, so did she and so did I,
And the more I think about it sure the nearer I am to cry,
Oh, wasn't it the happy times when troubles we had not,
And our mothers made Colcannon in the little skillet pot.

Did you ever bring potato cake in a basket to the school,
Tucked underneath your arm with your book, your slate and rule,
And when teacher wasn't looking sure a great big bite you'd take,
Of the flowery flavoured buttered soft and sweet potato cake.

Did you ever go a-courting as the evening sun went down,
And the moon began a-peeping from behind the Hill o' Down,
As you wandered down the boreen where the leprechaun was seen,
And you whispered loving phrases to your little fair colleen.

GOING TO MARKET.

OMB 76

Galway Bay

By A. Cohalan

If you e-ver go a-cross the sea to Ire - land, Then may-be at the clos-ing of your day. You will sit and watch the moon rise o-ver Clad - dagh, And see the sun go down on Gal-way Bay.

Just to hear again the ripple of the trout stream,
The women in the meadows making hay,
And to sit beside a turf-fire in the cabin,
And to watch the barefoot Gossoons at their play.

For the breezes blowing o'er the seas from Ireland,
Are perfumed by the heather as they blow,
And the women in the uplands diggin' praties,
Speak a language that the strangers do not know.

For the strangers came and tried to teach us their way,
They scorn'd us just for being what we are,
But they might as well go chasing after moonbeams,
Or light a penny candle from a star.

And if there is going to be a life hereafter,
And somehow I am sure there's going to be,
I will ask God to let me make my heaven,
In that dear land across the Irish Sea.

The Castle of Dromore

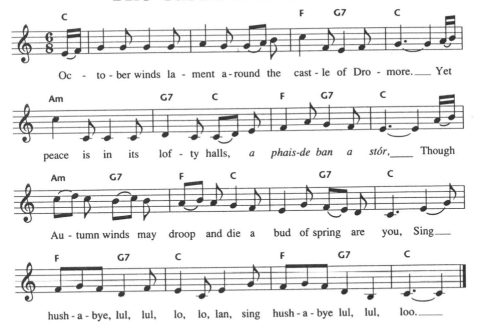

Oc - to - ber winds la - ment a - round the cast - le of Dro - more.___ Yet

peace is in its lof - ty halls, *a phais-de ban a stór,*___ Though

Au - tumn winds may droop and die a bud of spring are you, Sing___

hush - a - bye, lul, lul, lo, lo, lan, sing hush - a - bye lul, lul, loo.___

Bring no ill wind to hinder us, my helpless babe and me -
Dread spirit of Blackwater banks, Clan Eoin's wild banshee,
And Holy Mary pitying, in heaven for grace doth sue,
Sing hushabye, lul, lul, lo, lo, lan,
Sing hushabye, lul, lul, loo.

Take time to thrive, my Rose of hope, in the garden of Dromore;
Take heed young Eagle - till your wings are weathered fit to soar;
A little time and then our land is full of things to do,
Sing hushabye, lul, lul, lo, lo, lan,
Sing hushabye, lul, lul, loo.

My Lagan Love

Where La - gan stream sings lull - a - bye, there blows a li - ly fair,

the twi - light gleam is in her eye, the night____ is on her hair,

and like a love - sick len - an - shee, she____ hath my heart____ in thrall;

Nor life I owe, nor li - ber - ty, for love____ is lord of all.

And often when the beetle's horn
Hath lulled her eye to sleep,
I steal unto her shieling lorn
And thro' the dooring peep;
There on the cricket's singing stone
She stirs the bog-wood fire,
And hums in sad, sweet undertone
The song of heart's desire.

Her welcome like her love for me
Is from the heart within.
Her warm kiss is felicity
That knows no taint or sin.
When she was only fairy small,
Her gentle mother died.
But true love keeps her memory warm
By Lagan's silver side.

Old Woman from Wexford

There was an old wo-man from Wex - ford, in Wex - ford she did dwell, She

loved her hus - band dear - ly, but an - o - ther man twice as well With me

rum a dum dum   a   de - ro, and   me   dum   a - de - ro - dee.____

One day she went to the doctor, some medicine for to find,
She said 'Will you give me something, that will make my old man blind.'
CHORUS

'Feed him eggs and marrow bones and make him suck them all,
And it won't be very long after, till he won't see you at all.'
CHORUS

The doctor wrote a letter and he signed it with his hand,
And he sent it to the old man, just to make him understand.
CHORUS

So she fed him eggs and marrow bones and made him suck them all,
And it wasn't very long after till he couldn't see the wall.
CHORUS

He said 'I'll go and drown myself but I fear it is a sin,'
Says she, 'I'll go along with you and help to push you in.'
CHORUS

The woman she stepped back a bit to rush and push him in,
But the old man quietly stepped aside and she went tumbling in.
CHORUS

Oh how loudly she did yell and how loudly she did call,
'Yerra, hold your whist, old woman,' says he.
CHORUS

So eggs are eggs and marrow bones may make your old man blind,
But if you want to drown him, you must creep up close behind.
CHORUS

OMB 76

The Star of the County Down

Near to Ban - bridge town, in the coun - ty Down, one morn - ing in Ju - ly, Down a bo - reen green came a sweet col - leen and she smiled as she passed me by; Oh, she looked so neat from her two white feet, to the sheen of her nut - brown hair, Sure the coax - ing elf, I'd to shake my - self, to make sure I was stand - ding there. Oh from Ban - try Bay up to Der - ry Quay, and from Gal - way to Dub - lin town, No maid I've seen like the sweet col - leen, that I met in the coun - ty Down.

As she onward sped I shook my head
And I gazed with a feeling quare,
'And I said', says I to a passer-by
'Who's the maid with the nut-brown hair?'
Oh he smiled at me, and with pride says he:
'That's the gem of Ireland's crown,
She's young Rosie McCann, from the banks of the Bann,
She's the star of the County Down'.

She'd a soft brown eye and a look so sly
And a smile like the rose in June,
And you hung on each note from her lily-white throat,
As she lilted an Irish tune.
At the pattern dance you were held in trance
As she tripped through a reel or a jig,
And when her eyes she'd roll, she'd coax upon my soul
A spud from a hungry pig.

I've travelled a bit, but never was hit,
Since my roving career began;
But fair and square I surrendered thee
To the charm of young Rosie McCann
With a heart to let and no tenant yet,
Did I meet within shawl or gown.
But in she went and I asked no rent
From the star of the County Down.

At the crossroads fair I'll be surely there
And I'll dress in my Sunday clothes,
And I'll try sheep's eyes and deludhering lies
On the heart of the nut-brown Rose.
No pipe I smoke, no horse I'll yoke
Though my plough with rust turns brown
Till a smiling bride by my own fireside
Sits the star of the County Down.

Lisburn.

OMB 76

Handsome Sally

Young men and maid - ens I pray draw near; the
truth to you I will now de - clare, How a young la - dy's___
heart was won, All___ by the lo - ving of a far - mer's son.

As she walked out through a silent grove,
Who should she meet but her true love.
'Kind Sir,' she said,'And upon my life,
I do intend to be your wife.'

'Oh, fairest creature it cannot be
That I should be wedded unto thee.
Since I am going for to be wed
To Handsome Sally your waiting maid.'

'If that be true as you tell to me,
A bitter pill I will prove to thee,
For shipping I'll take immediately
And I'll sail with Sally to Floridee.'

As they were sailing upon the Main,
This wicked wretch she contrived a scheme:
While handsome Sally lay fast asleep,
She plunged her body into the deep.

Hanged and burned then was she,
For her sad crime and cruelty.
So two fair maids were by love undone,
And in Bedlam lies the farmer's son.

Reilly's Daughter

As I was sit-ting by the fire, talk-ing to old Reil-ly's daugh-ter

sud-den-ly a thought came in-to my head: I'd like to mar-ry old Reil-ly's daugh-ter,

Chorus

Gid-dy-I Ay, Gid-dy-I Ay, Gid-dy-I Ay for the one-eyed Reil-ly,

Gid-dy-I Ay, bang, bang, bang, play it on your big brass drum.

For Reilly played on the big brass drum
Reilly had a mind for murder and slaughter
Reilly had a bright red glittering eye,
And he kept that eye on his lovely daughter.

Her hair was black and her eyes were blue
The colonel and the major and the captain sought her
The sergeant and the private and the drummer boy, too,
But they never had a chance with O'Reilly's daughter.

I got me a ring and a parson too,
I got me a 'scratch' in the married quarter
Settled me down to a peaceful life,
As happy as a king with O'Reilly's daughter.

Suddenly a footstep on the stair,
Who should it be but the one-eyed Reilly
With two pistols in his hand
Looking for the man who married his daughter.

I took O'Reilly by the hair,
Rammed his head in a pail of water,
Fired his pistols in the air,
A darned sight quicker than I married his daughter.

OMB 76

Red is the Rose

Come o - ver the hills, my bon - nie I - rish
Chorus Red is the rose that in yon - der gar - den

lass, Come o - ver the hills to your dar - ling,
grows And fair is the li - ly of the val - ley,

You choose the rose love, and I'll____ make the vow, And
Clear is the wa - ter that flows____ from the Boyne, But

I'll be your true love for e - ver.____
my love is fair - er than a - ny.____

'Twas down by Killarney's green woods that we strayed,
And the moon and the stars they were shining,
The moon shone its rays on her locks of golden hair,
And she swore she'd be my love forever.

It's not for the parting that my sister pains,
It's not for the grief of my mother,
'Tis all for the loss of my bonnie Irish lass,
That my heart is breaking forever.

Sweet Carnloch Bay

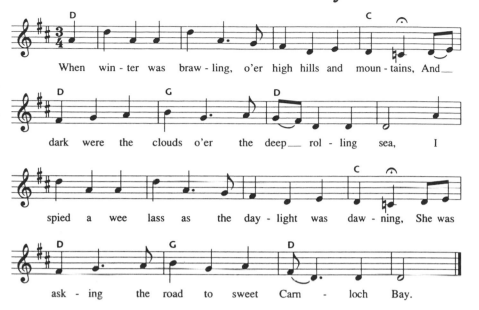

When win-ter was braw-ling, o'er high hills and moun-tains, And dark were the clouds o'er the deep rol-ling sea, I spied a wee lass as the day-light was daw-ning, She was ask-ing the road to sweet Carn-loch Bay.

I said, 'My wee lassie, I canna weel tell ye
The number of miles or how far it might be,
But if you'll consent I'll convoy you a wee bit,
And I'll show you the road to sweet Carnloch Bay.

You turn to the right and pass down by the churchyard
Cross over the river and down by the sea;
We'll call in Pat Hamill's and have a wee drop there
Just to help us along to sweet Carnloch Bay.'

Here's a health to Pat Hamill likewise the wee lassie
And to every laddie that's listening to me
And ne'er turn your back on a bonnie wee lassie
When she's asking the road to sweet Carnloch Bay.

OMB 76

Paddy's Green Shamrock Shore

Oh fare - thee well to Ire_____ land, my
own dear na - tive land_____ It breaks my
heart to see friends part. For it's then that the
tear drops fall._____ I'm on my way to
A - me - ri - kay. Will I e - ver see home once
more._____ For now I leave my own true
love. And Pad - dy's Green Sham - rock Shore._____

From Londonderry we did sail, it being on the fourth of May,
Pleasant weather I'm sure we had going to America.
Fresh water then we did take in, one hundred tons or more,
For fear we'd be short on the other side, far from the Shamrock Shore.

Two of our anchors we did weigh before we left the quay,
Down the river we were towed till we came to Botany Bay.
We saw that night the grandest night we ever saw before,
The sun going down 'tween sea and sky far from the Shamrock Shore.

Early next morning we were sea-sick all, not one of us was free.
I, myself was confined to bed with no one to pity me;
No father or no mother to raise my head when sore;
That made me think of the friends I left on the lonely Shamrock Shore.

We landed safely in New York after four and twenty days,
Each comrade by the hand we took and we marched through different ways.
Each one drank a flowing glass as we might meet no more,
With flowing bumpers we drank a health to the lonely Shamrock shore.

Market of the Claddagh Fishermen.

OMB 76

The Raggle Taggle Gypsies

Three gyp - sies stood at the cas - tle gate, They
sang so high, they sang so low, The la - dy sat in her
cham - ber late, Her heart it mel - ted a - way as snow.

They sang so sweet, they sang so shrill,
That fast her tears began to flow,
And she laid down her silken gown,
Her golden rings and all her show.

She pluck-ed off her high-heeled shoes,
A-made of Spanish leather, O
She went in the street with her bare, bare feet;
All out in the wind and weather, O.

O saddle to me my milk-white steed,
And go and fetch my pony, O
That I may ride and seek my bride,
Who is gone with the raggle taggle gypsies, O.

O he rode high and he rode low,
He rode through wood and copses, too,
Until he came to an open field,
And there he espied his lady, O.

What makes you leave your house and land,
Your golden treasures for to go,
What makes you leave your new-wedded lord
To follow the raggle taggle gypsies, O.

What care I for my house and land
What care I for my treasure, O,
What care I for my newly-wedded lord,
I'm off with the raggle taggle gypsies, O.

Last night you slept on a goose-feather bed,
With the sheets turned down so bravely, O,
And to-night you shall sleep in a cold open field,
Along with the raggle taggle gypsies, O.

What care I for a goose-feather bed
With the sheet turned down so bravely, O,
For to-night I shall sleep in a cold open field,
Along with the raggle taggle gypsies, O.

My Singing Bird

I have seen the lark soar high at morn to sing up in the blue, I have

heard the black - bird pipe its song, the thrush and the lin - net too. But

none of them can sing so sweet, my sing - ing bird as you, Aah __

__ My sing - ing bird as you.

If I could lure my singing bird from its own cosy nest,
If I could catch my singing bird I would warm it on my breast,
And on my heart my singing bird would sing itself to rest,
Aah . . . . Would sing itself to rest.

Kinsale Harbor.

39

OMB 76

The Rose of Mooncoin

By S. Kavanagh

How sweet 'tis to roam by the sun-ny Suir stream, And hear the dove coo 'neath the morn-ing sun-beam, Where the thrush and the rob-in their sweet notes en-twine. On the banks of the Suir that flows down by Moon-coin.

Chorus

Flow on, love-ly riv-er flow gent-ly a-long. By your wa-ters so sweet sounds the lark's mer-ry song. On your green banks I'll wan-der where first I did join With you love-ly Mol-ly, the Rose of Moon-coin.

Oh! Molly, dear Molly, it breaks my fond heart
To know that we two for ever must part.
I'll think of you, Molly, while sun and moon shine
On the banks of the Suir that flows down by Mooncoin.

She has sailed far away o'er the dark rolling foam
Far away from the hills of her dear Irish home
Where the fisherman sports with his small boat and line
On the banks of the Suir that flows down by Mooncoin.

Then here's to the Suir with its valleys so fair
As oft' times we wandered in the cool morning air
Where the roses are blooming and lilies entwine
On the banks of the Suir that flows down by Mooncoin.

HOLY CROSS ABBEY, TIPPERARY.

OMB 76

Lanigan's Ball

In the town of A-thy one Je-re-my La-ni-gan bat-tered a-way till he
had-n't a pound, His fat-her he died and made him a man a-gain
left him a farm and ten a-cres of ground, He gave a grand par-ty to
friends and re-la-tions, Who did not for-get him when come to the wall,
If you but list-en, I'll make your eyes glist-en at the rows and ruc-tions of
La-ni-gan's ball.

Chorus

Six long months I spent in Dub-lin,
Six long months do-ing no-thing at all Six long months I
spent in Dub-lin, lear-ning to dance for La-ni-gan's ball. I stepped out,
I stepped in a-gain, I stepped out a-gain, I stepped in a-gain, I stepped out and
I stepped in a-gain, lear-ning to dance for La-ni-gan's ball.

Myself to be sure got free invitations,
For all the nice girls and boys I might ask.
And just in a minute both friends and relations
Were dancing as merry as bees round a cask.
There was lashings of punch and wine for the ladies,
Potatoes and cakes, there was bacon and tea,
There were the Nolans, the Dolans, O'Gradys,
Courting the girls and dancing away.

They were doing all kinds of nonsensical polkas,
All round the room in a whirligig,
But Julia and I soon banished their nonsense
And tipped them a twist of a real Irish jig.
Oh, how that girl got mad on me,
And danced till you'd think the ceilings would fall,
For I spent three weeks at Brooks Academy
Learning to dance for Lanigan's Ball.

Repeat chorus but add:

I stepped out, I stepped in again,
I stepped in again and I stepped out again,
I stepped out, I stepped in again,
Learning to dance for Lanigan's Ball.

The boys were as merry, the girls all hearty,
Dancing away in couples and groups,
Till an accident happened; young Terence Mc Carthy,
He put his right leg through Miss Finnerty's hoops.
The creature she fainted and cried 'Meelia, murther'
Called for her brothers and gathered them all,
Carmody swore that he'd go no further,
Till he'd have satisfaction at Lanigan's Ball.

In the midst of the row, Miss Kerrigan fainted,
Her cheeks at the same time as red as a rose,
Some of the boys decried she was painted
She took a small drop too much, I suppose.
Her sweetheart Ned Morgan, so powerful and able,
When he saw his fair colleen stretched by the wall,
He tore the left leg from under the table
And smashed all the dishes at Lanigan's Ball.

Boys, oh boys 'tis then there was ructions
Myself got a kick from big Phelim Mc Hugh,
But soon I replied to his kind introduction
And kicked up a terrible hullabaloo.
Ould Casey, the piper, was near being strangled,
They squeezed up his pipes, bellows, chanters and all.
The girls in their ribbons they all got entangled,
And that put an end to Lanigan's Ball.

OMB 76

Moorlough Mary

When first I saw my Moor-lough Ma-ry 'twas at the mar-ket of sweet Stra-bane, Her thril-ling glanc-es were so en-ga-ging, the hearts of young men she did tre-pan. Her thril-ling glan-ces be-reft my sen-ses, Of peace and com-fort ei-ther night or day, In si-lent slum-ber I turn and mur-mur, "Oh Moor-lough Ma-ry won't you come a-way?"

Were I a man of great education
And Erin's Isle at my command,
I'd lay my head on your throbbing bosom,
In wedlock bands, love, we'd join our hands.
I'd entertain you both night and morning
With robes I'd deck you both fine and gay
And with kisses, sweet love, I would caress you.
Oh Moorlough Mary, won't you come away?

I marched away to my situation,
My recreation was all in vain
On the river Mourne where the salmon are sporting
And the rocks re-echoing their plaintive strain.
The thrush and blackbird would sing so sweetly
With notes melodious on the river brae,
And the little song-birds would sing in chorus
Oh Moorlough Mary, won't you come away?

Then fare thee well to my Moorlough Mary
Ten thousand times I bid you adieu,
While breath remains in my throbbing bosom,
I will never cease, love, to think of you.
I marched away to some lonesome valley
With tears a-flowing both night and day,
In some silent harbour, where none shall hear me,
Oh Moorlough Mary, won't you come away?

Rock and Ruins of Cashel.

OMB 76

The Glendalough Saint

In Glen-da-lough lived an old saint, re-nowned for his learn-ing and pie-ty,___ His man-ners were cu-rious and quaint,___ and he looked u-pon girls with dis-pa-ri-ty, Ri fol di dol, fol di dol day,___ Ri fol di dol, fol di dol lad-dy,___ Ri fol di dol, fol di dol day,___ Ri fol di dol, fol di dol lad-dy.

But as he was fishin' one day,
A-catchin' some kind of trout, sir,
Young Kathleen was walkin' that way
Just to see what the saint was about, sir.
'You're a mighty fine fisher', says Kate,
'Tis yourself is the boy that can hook them,
But when you have caught them so nate,
Don't you want some young woman to cook them?'

'Be gone out of that', said the saint,
'For I am a man of great piety,
Me character I wouldn't taint,
By keeping such class of society.'
But Kathleen wasn't goin' to give in,
For when he got home to his rockery,
He found her sitting therein,
A-polishing up of his crockery.

He gave the poor creature a shake,
Oh, I wish that the peelers had caught him;
He threw her right into the lake,
And of course she sank down to the bottom.
It is rumoured from that very day,
Kathleen's ghost can be seen on the river;
And the saint never raised up his hand,
For he died of the right kind of fervour.

GLENDALOUGH.

47

The Well Below the Valley

A gent - le - man was pas - sing by, he asked a drink as he got dry, at this well be - low the val - ley -O, Green grows the li - ly -O, right a - mong the bush - es -O, I'll be se - ven years a - ring - ing a bell but the Lord a - bove may save my soul from por - tin in hell, at the well be - low the val - ley - O.

She said 'my cup it overflows,
If I stoop down I might fall in,'
At the well below the valley-o.

If your true love was passing by,
You'd fill him a drink if he got dry
At the well below the valley-o.

She swore by grass, she swore by corn,
That her true love was never born,
At the well below the valley-o.

I say, young maid, you're swearing wrong,
For five fine children you had born
At the well below the valley-o.

If you're a man of noble fame,
You'll tell me who's the father of them,
At the well below the valley-o.

OMB 76

There was two of them by your uncle Dan,
Another two by your brother John,
At the well below the valley-o.

Another by your father dear
At the well below the valley-o,
At the well below the valley-o.

Well if you're a man of noble fame,
You'll tell me what did happen to them,
At the well below the valley-o.

There was two of them buried by the stable door,
Another two 'neath the kitchen floor,
At the well below the valley-o.

Another's buried by the well,
At the well below the valley-o,
At the well below the valley-o.

Well if you're a man of noble fame,
You'll tell me what will happen myself
At the well below the valley-o.

You'll be seven years a-porterin in hell,
And seven years a-ringing a bell,
At the well below the valley-o.

I'll be seven years a-ringing a bell
But the Lord above may save my soul from portin' in hell,
At the well below the valley-o.

The Meeting of the Waters

By Thomas Moore

There is not in the wide world a val - ley so sweet, As that vale in whose bo - som the bright wa - ters meet, Oh! the last rays of feel - ing and life must de - part. Ere the bloom of that val - ley shall fade from my heart! Ere the bloom of that val - ley shall fade from my heart.

'Twas that friends, the beloved of my bosom, were near,
Who made every dear scene of enchantment more dear
And who felt how the best charms of Nature improve
When we see them reflected from looks that we love.

Sweet vale of Avoca! How calm could I rest
In thy bosom of shade, with the friends I love best;
Where the storms that we feel in this cold world should cease,
And our hearts, like thy waters, be mingled in peace.

She Moved Through the Fair

My young love said to me,____ "My moth - er won't mind____

____ And my fath - er won't slight you for your lack of kine."____

____ And she stepp'd a - way from me and this she did say:____ "It

will not be long love____ till our wed - ding . day."____

She stepped away from me and she moved through the fair,
And fondly I watched her go here and go there,
Then she went her way homeward with one star awake,
As the swan in the evening moves over the lake.

The people were saying no two were e'er wed,
But one has a sorrow that never was said,
And I smiled as she passed with her goods and her gear,
And that was the last that I saw of my dear.

I dreamt it last night that my young love came in,
So softly she entered, her feet made no din,
She came close beside me and this she did say,
'It will not be long love, till our wedding day.'

OMB 76

The Bard of Armagh

Oh, list to the lay of a poor Irish harper, and scorn not the strains of his withered old hand, Remember his fingers, they once could move sharper, To raise up the mem-'ry of his dear native land.

When I was a young lad King Jamie did flourish
And I followed the wars in my brogues bound with straw.
And all the fair colleens from Wexford to Durrish
Called me bold Phelim Brady, the Bard of Armagh.

How I love for to muse on the days of my boyhood
Tho' four score and three years have flitted since then,
Still it gives sweet reflections as every young joy should,
For light-hearted boys to make the best of old men.

At pattern of fair I could twist my shillelagh
Or trip through the jig with my brogues bound with straw,
Whilst all the pretty maidens around me assembled
Loving bold Phelim Brady, the Bard of Armagh.

Although I have travelled this wide world over,
Yet Erin's a home and a parent to me;
Then, oh, let the ground that my old bones shall cover
Be cut from the soil that is trod by the free.

And when Sergeant Death in his cold arms shall embrace me,
Oh, lull me to sleep with 'Erin go Bragh',
By the side of my Kathleen, my young wife, oh, place me,
Then forget Phelim Brady, the Bard of Armagh.

Armagh.

53

The Holy Ground

A - dieu, my fair young mai - den, A thous - and times a - dieu____ we must bid fare - well to the Ho - ly Ground and the girls that we love true.____ We will sail the salt sea o - ver and re - turn a - gain for sure,____ To seek the girls who wait for us in the Ho - ly Ground once more. FINE GIRL YOU ARE,____ You're the girl that I a - dore____ And still I live in hopes to see the Ho - ly Ground once __ more, FINE GIRL YOU ARE____

Oh the night was dark and stormy,
You scarce could see the moon,
And our good old ship was tossed about,
And her rigging was all torn;
With her seams agape and leaky,
With her timbers dozed and old,
And still I live in hopes to see
The Holy Ground once more.

And now the storm is over,
And we are safe on shore,
Let us drink a health to the Holy Ground
And the girls that we do adore;
We will drink strong ale and porter
Till we make the taproom roar
And when our money all is spent
We will go to sea for more.

The Jug of Punch

'Twas ve - ry ear - ly in the month of June, as I was sit - ting
in my room I heard a thrush sing in a bush and the song it
sang was the jug of punch.___ *Chorus* Too - ra - loo - ra - loo, too - ra - loo - ra -
loo, too - ra - loo - ra - loo, too - ra - loo - ra - loo, I heard a thrush
sing in a bush and the song it sang was the Jug of Punch.___

What more diversion can a man desire.
Than to be seated by a snug coal fire,
Upon his knee a pretty wench
And on the table a jug of punch

If I were sick and very bad,
And was not able to go or stand,
I would not think it all amiss,
To pledge my shoes for a jug of punch.

The doctor fails with all his art,
To cure an impression on the heart,
But if life was gone, within an inch,
What would bring it back but a jug of punch.

But when I'm dead and in my grave,
No costly tombstone I will have,
But they'll dig a grave both wide and deep,
With a jug of punch at my head and feet.

OMB 76

Publisher's Note :
The majority of songs included in this collection follow the same format of
our well-known *'Folksongs and Ballads Popular in Ireland'* by John Loesberg.
'Folksongs and Ballads' however features no less than 200 songs within the
four volumes available. Information on the origins of each song is also
included.

Folksongs and Ballads Popular in Ireland, Volume 1
collected, edited and arranged by John Loesberg
(OMB 1)
Folksongs and Ballads Popular in Ireland, Volume 2
(OMB 2)
Folksongs and Ballads Popular in Ireland, Volume 3
(OMB 3)
Folksongs and Ballads Popular in Ireland, Volume 4
(OMB 4)

Ossian Publications produce a huge range of Irish Music,
ranging from Sheetmusic, Songbooks, Tune Collections,
Instruction Books to an acclaimed catalogue of
Traditional Irish Music on Cassette tapes and CD's.
For a complete list of all our publications please send your
name and address together with an (international)
Postal Reply Coupon to;

•**Ossian Publications Ltd.**•
P.O.Box 84, Cork, Ireland